BEARINGS

BEARINGS

poems by JACK MARSHALL

HARPER & ROW, PUBLISHERS
NEW YORK, EVANSTON,
AND LONDON

1817

Acknowledgment is made to the following publications, in which some of these poems have previously appeared: *Epoch, Poetry, Niobe, For Now, Analecta, El Corno Emplumado, The Hudson Review, The Darkest Continent,* and *Vincent, Mad Brother of Theo.* The poems "Hitch-Hiker," "Setting Out," and "Bearings" appeared originally in *The New Yorker.*

FIRST EDITION

LIBRARY OF CONGRESS CATALOG CARD NUMBER: 70-81878

For Kathleen and David

CONTENTS

I. FORCED ENTRY

FORCED ENTRY   11

CIANO   12

CONNECTIONS   13

THE FEEDING MACHINE   14

THE LADY IS MY LANGUAGE   15

FOR SILENCE   16

WHITE SPIDERS   17

EL JEFE   18

FOR A SPIRIT UNBORN   20

II. LINES FOR A HARVEST

LINES FOR A HARVEST   27

CHORUSES FROM UNDER THE GREEN UMBRELLA   28

THAW   31

CYCLE FOR SERGIO   32

SKY OVER MEXICO   35

ON THE PRESIDENT'S STATE VISIT TO MEXICO   38

WORDS OVERHEARD IN AN APPLE ORCHARD   40

BACON'S VAN GOGH   41

THE FOUNDRY   42

III. MY TROPICS

MY TROPICS   47

FOR A GENTLEMAN WITH BLEACHED HAIR   49

HITCH-HIKER   51

ARMOR   52

WALKING ACROSS BROOKLYN BRIDGE   53

FOR KATHLEEN, GONE ON A BRIEF JOURNEY   55

WALKING ON A CLEAR DAY   56

I HAD COME TO HOPE FOR SOMETHING   58

LEAVING THE HOSPITAL   60

IN NO TIME   64

IV. SETTING OUT

SETTING OUT   67

BEARINGS   68

THE ANGEL   69

FOR A NEW HOUSE   71

CHANGES   72

POEM   76

THE VISIT   78

LIGHT POEM   80

GOING OUT TO MEET THE SUN IN A TIME OF DARKNESS   81

YOU ARE WATER   82

REMAINS   83

I Forced Entry

FORCED ENTRY

With its foot in the door of your head
With its drop of light
With its bunch of flowers   of grass   of sea-spray
With its oil of sexual fish
With the beginnings of corruption   with shameless laughter
With its blast of desire
With its taste for your salt-lipped beauty
With its silence
With its window that says Casa
With its buds opening like Chinese flowers

                                    around ancient cities

With its vibration of an African drum
With its blackbird flown to Vera Cruz
With its lion cub roped to a tree
With its clipped wings
With its valise full of travel posters
With its hatred of metals
With its cutting edge
With its submarine of survivors
With its flagpole that has run down all flags
With its shape of a grave-digger's shovel
With its vein of ore
With its speed of a runner who leaves no tracks

        I jab into your mouth, this poem, this tongue.

CIANO

Say what say a hunk of bones
too busy land-grabbing
to know the lies, the lies
shoveled higher than we care to know
made a pact with her the heavy eater
for his silence she'd let him off her plate
still some knowledge gone into exile
ripened in silence will rot the air
in the streets and boulevards that bear her name
the badlands of Patagonia   the gasmask of the moon
glowing in his head and no use saying
you'll have no part in it   you will
big fat sheriff rusted hunk of tin
tied to life as to four horses
feel your knees give up the shelter of their sockets
hear the cries by the brink of the marsh
by the water-wheels in the white dust of Ethiopia
and never out of range   the tsetse formations in the haze
denying themselves no pleasure
a growth clear as gin   flaming outward
a legionnaire legs deliciously round his charger
rides forward bearing on his lance a piece of scarlet cloth
the dawn of a grand era   the balls of his victim

CONNECTIONS

— for Murray

Rant, retreat, rally of energies
shifting gears, strung out
singing across what icy temperatures
across what outrushing gas of stars
    What time shall I set my watch to
    What trade it for
        or live in, whole, this skin
        dazed at the sight of its own astronomy?
    Butcherings I don't dare except in dreams
        explode in my face as headlines
            Darkness,
            rings of darkness
            in me O
                I lay on you

THE FEEDING MACHINE

He is shaking the tree on which you grow
my love, shaking the tree with fury,
and as you toss you think it's the play
of the south breeze in no hurry.

He is picking you up from the earth
my love, picking you like an apple;
that is your flesh between his teeth,
that's a bayonet on his table.

He is biting into your skin
my love, skin so soft and trusting,
bites till your bones cave in,
and skewers your cheeks for basting.

He is chewing you into pieces
my love, his chewing jaw like a harrow;
when he swallows he'll leave no trace
oh, and no seed for tomorrow.

THE LADY IS MY LANGUAGE

The lady is my language
I'll let the images go bare
Images of velvet and brilliantined hair
The lady's my language
When I can't make do with despair

Oh one for the money
Two to show
A kitestring could strangle
Everything I know

There's safety in numbers
There's courage in crowds
The bombers move closer
In the beautiful clouds
If all the flowers are dropped in the sea
I'll let her blue eyes speak for me

This lady, my language
She's running like a sheep
From two drunken soldiers
In a camouflaged jeep
She's barefoot
I watch her being raped in my sleep

Watch her hollow eyes speak for me.

FOR SILENCE

In the era of maximum darkness when Light, the Angel
    that was to show Himself, didn't;
In the era when the shrill Kabuki cry shot upward
    from a voice of sand burned to glass, a crystal butterfly
    whose wing-dust had been blown off;
In the era when Language spread her papery legs
    and did an obscene cancan on billboards across the prairie;
In the era when letters of the alphabet ballooned from our mouths,
    becoming a cloud of locusts blocking out the sun . . .

> . . . a little light please,
> a sandgrain,
> silence.

Let the heaviness of noise fall from me like handfuls of hair,
    like a skin of insects, a set of teeth,
    like my body sliding off yours cools all of summer's madness;
Let the walls of noise crumble in a final demolition
    of temples, palaces, pyramids, skyscrapers, prisons;
Let the rich suits of noise be chewed to a silken dust
    by a cosmic release of moths;
Let the appliances of noise be served up like hearts
    on a black stone in the Temple of the Sun.

Oh my cold white, salt frozen angels,
Man is a city blaring with red alarms;
Let his throat be a highway
    on which nothing but your light feet walk
                cutting off his speech.

WHITE SPIDERS

They are so old, lord, and bleached so white
Siamese thriving side by side, like mushrooms
In fours and sixes leeching to the back seats
Wizened wax cadavers
smelling of drugstore powder, the sex dried out. . . .

Oh lord, how they shrivel under hair-dryers
while the roaring black sun of the world bloats,
bloats and will burst close at hand
and send forth what new stars. . . .

Everywhere the moist green earth's erotic eye
opens, they rush to buy it up and board it,
deadweight thread of our lives run through a spinning wheel
Old Martha's ambitious fingers
spinning white web of these states
now the Spider . . .

                    So still they are,
and clutch stillness to their bosoms like a purse;
stillness of the iguana slit open,
black snap of its watchful eye,
these crones too slow too sure of nothing that is not in them
to see it move a notch closer, blink and swallow.

EL JEFE

Past midnight and he's still up
nursing his third Scotch and soda,
watching the coded messages snake along the floor
like a cobra swaying to his tune,
in a wing of the star whose light we live on,
not flickering blue or red shifting out of sight, but white;
white as the livery of a footman, the sheen of a tablecloth;
white as a blank check;
white as a motor that purrs to the touch;
white as newsprint about to be blackened;
white as a hallway clicking with jackboots;
white as the flash of an explosion. . . .

And he sits in the center of the star fallen into the Potomac,
his fist full of telegrams he worries over
like doctors over a heartbeat,
and his flock, snoring away their back-talk in the warmth of the fold
he is sworn to protect and prolong into another generation
blessed with obedience, and another and another,
till the whole earth swells with well-wishers—

He wants to be out there with his boys, riding
in the cockpit where bright moonglow boils down
to where night is the enemy,
night that has designs on us, and in us,

                                        wipe it out!

It is dark, it deceives, it prowls on its belly,
it is not white.
Light up the blackness with the radiance of G.E.;
anything that moves in it moves against us;
we cannot rest or cease or sleep
till the world is ablaze with searchlights
outstaring the nightmare that flies low as we wake.

FOR A SPIRIT UNBORN

Is it because we are too suddenly beautiful
that the old sun can't take it,
falling in on us,
grinding the fleshy grain colorless

                as a meal of ashes?

      Is it because we are!

O surplus of Isaacs!—
O cowed fathers
whose silence hovers like a knife—
on this hard ground near freezing,
beneath these gold-brewing trees,
I grab hold of the ancient club—

                  my throat—
the one weapon you could not wrench from me—
and prepare to win back each blade
of grass.

        I mobilize whole war-painted forests!
A day is all history

            and the end

                of history.

         I am the first

        day of creation, the father of nations!
I will not slow down my progress
with sudden pangs of mercy
for the children broken from their stalks, or flowers in rags
blowing across borders,
like refugees.

The sea is here,
the odor of the sea is still
here . . .
it's someone else that's missing!

Summer in its small ways was violent.

Autumn, O quarter of blood,
no use to look back with longing
at a waning sun,
when the light we are tracking
has nothing to do with the false
glow of childhood.

O rag-ends of maroon and emerald,
what nation is like you!
How you come through
when my joy demands to be dazzled
like a tyrant!
What wounds more fabulous at the height
of fall!

The soaked leaves
sponge off the bloodied face
and draw it down.

Is it because I am locked
with my friends in a desperate embrace,
or that desire is keener
for being held so close to the flame,
that love takes on a shine
like violence!

Faithful enemies, secret agitators, my nuances,
friends!—let us use one another
in a new kind of war,
where the strong will learn to tremble
and the weak to laugh, powerful with contradictions!

With life still a dry gurgle in their throats,
we'll leave our slaves clinging
to the dried-up tits of desert midwives;
we'll leave peace
to sink its unwieldy apes like dinosaurs in the swamps
of cities.

We'll leave each other, perfected lovers of ourselves.

I will create a dissonant jazz
of the grunts
                    and animal cries
of a woman's face twisted in labor—a sound
to be felt with the eye!
I'll be decked out
in the red satin pageboy suit of my original fever.
I will announce a great contempt for the century!—
what makes it think I am its fellow-man?
How does it know I am not
                    a dark continent!
I'll speak only curses!
I won't speak!
                    What drug is purer than I!

That turbulence at your throat . . . swallow
its frenzy; feel it
filling out the future like a spinnaker
                              breaking
to where everything is a mingling of chaos and discovery. . . .

Ah, then we will know, truly and simply,
how to inherit the earth.

II   Lines for a Harvest

LINES FOR A HARVEST

Down, down and down the orchards bend
to the turned valley's cobble.
Almonds in their green cartridges break
white and sweet; grapevines, like rough lovers,
twine in rows, and terra cotta
the dry riverbed gleams—reptilian backbone
moving toward water through the morning haze.

Everything smells of life,
as though the earth had emerged
from a great rain. . . .
even the iron tools, caked
and cool in a dark corner of the shed.

Yet something in me weighs untended.
And when the feet that pressed the grapes
have slipped back into their shoes,
and downhill the red stain trails
them to their door,
deep in the smallest bone of my skull
shall lie, curled in armor, a snail,
stalk-eyes nippling for sun.

CHORUSES FROM UNDER THE GREEN UMBRELLA

1.

Returning Autumn discovers
the gritty butterfly;
ritual appears to have begun
beautifully,
bitterness whistling somewhere.
Someone, waiting, slithers down,
softly sleeping,
becomes the road.

2.

Everywhere, the air priming.
Huns happen
in streetclothes, listen.
Goodbye wheelchair,
smooth wings play the sound of
home.

3.

Christmas, my pride,
hand me down the drum.
Unhappiness, chimeras say so too.
Astonishing cow-bells,
the lights of Bengal
flutter to the spectacle of lilacs
strewn under the table.

4.

Branches know the flavor
of very small ribs.
Everyone gets a holiday
but the Chinaman goes on pressing.
Love, a pot of lentils on a stove,
an ample library . . .
What if you can't get used to winter?
Rise up and romp in the red-faced wind.

5.

Shrink, father, to a pencil;
enmesh the hungry harem with mail;
cable from ship or Adirondack forest;
rejuvenate the ice machine
with an intake of clean dimes.

6.

The gaudy citizen, a billiard ball
with pockets full of plagues and poems,
lethal, refined, a kepi of knowledge;
neck up, a down-and-out sculpture
falters to the dance.

7.

Fighting to relieve the pain,
I held on tight,
hung around the railroad station,
dropped some pennies
in the dirty snows of the North,
and sweetly

days rolled off the rooftops,
dust rose to the stars.

8.

Sea is the background.
On the orange rim
tightrope walkers,
gracefully almond-shaped,
make strides toward the harvest.
The ringmaster is in black,
a shut figure.

THAW

It's like that in summer, the world
Cinctured by seas of wheat
And rough bands of wire
Framing a Breughel landscape.
Not the teeth in our wintry heads
Nor any part of us untouched.
Moss-green stones, night's flashbacks,
The seed of rich young men
Nozzled high in the air.
Orion's glassworks
Showering down in song, cinnabar and phlox.

CYCLE FOR SERGIO

1.

Tell of him on the rooftop under a radiant moon
in Mexico   oh slit-eyed guru   spread out
against white blowing sheets and infants' wear
The women   only piece of earth we get to know
taking hot showers   warming to love
"We are tied to the moon   its labors and losses
we shall never be free until we cut the tie

                       and connect to the sun

we are divorced from
always looking at   never out of"

2.

Plant yourself firmly in it   return
to this knowledge   that to die is to change
into flow of bubbling river   furrows
climbing into such a deep shade of green

                                  no single self
could come to on its own
And no need to set a time or place   wherever
in country of your birth

                         or sweating out exile
From under the ground you stand on
it knocks at your shoe-soles
the chestnut mare harnessed to the carob tree
carob tree corkscrewed in soil

                          laid on the hillside
and the hilltops are notches of your spine
where coruscations of sunlight beat a time not for keeping

      The tapeworm hangs in the still air
        its hook   a curve in the sun's greater circle

3.

So
cunningly
wrought—planes
and levels set back
between green terraces,
looking
up from
the base
is to watch the ascension of a soul
and not know where all that unfolding
leads to; heartbeat of the sun throbbing
in an arrowhead letting go of my death, the
serpent
Kundalini
uncoils
from the cellar of the human spine; from the graves
and garbage heaps of this ancient valley; a serpent
without thickness,   stretching   in columns   of stone;
trumpet without sound; unblinking eye; tripod of the gods;
mineshaft
vine
cock
of consciousness trying its full length somewhere beyond
my sight; a point of pure spirit wanting to take off and
join bird, water, the heat of the sun, the blowing wind;
the serpent of Being
uncoils
bright
as a
blossom

SKY OVER MEXICO

So slow in giving
or taking delight,
oh sad, near-sighted
optic of my soul,
that has seen half
the world purged
or pitching forward
with failing eyes
and not known which half
to throw in with . . .
here, where stone relics—
all mouth and belly—
squat in the red earth,
baking like ancestors,
I have come
as to a veiled woman,
without knowing, come
to find a match for
the pearled and towered
city that rides blue
as a second Venice on the water,
come to more of the same chase
only to slow down in the end
to a naked snail's pace
oozing homesickness.
My friends
are somewhere else,
in some hometown
I have kept my back to,
in a country, whole once,

now torn and tied in knots
by brute law and civil war.

Yet, mind and body
full of the weightless
sky blue grace,
will I knock and be let in
to each minute's thickness
like a ripe tomato?
Who or what will lead me
off this beaten path where
the giant candelabra cactus
lights a sky gone inky
as though not a God
but a god-like squid reigned above
and earth were not under heaven
but under water,
and nothing out of reach
of the assassin's ax or
the priest's sacrificial knife
or the swept-back teeth of the shark?

Still, someone, richer by a day,
lets the sun set in him
and closes a door;
another, discovering
a buried city in himself
begins unearthing a scroll, a tile,
and dreams
of a courtyard in Estremadura;
while in the kitchen,
the young Indian maid, remembering

some softer motion of her hips,
slips out to her lover,
and thrilled as any bird cry
flitting through the leaves,
her chirpy, cupped laughter
makes light
of all that dark sky.

Wait for morning, lean back, listen;
see the clouds bloom, folding
on all sides and cluster
a horizon of petals,
as though that bee
nosing the world for honey is me!
And down from the eucalyptus
on the hill's backbone,
from cracks in the blood-black
pyramids stacked with pyramids
of skulls to force-feed
the unimpregnable sun,
a fragrance of limes, of sweet
grass and stephanotis
cuts through layers of oil,
and whatever is green in me
swarms and surfaces to meet
this directionless
mint of freshness
suddenly thrown open.

ON THE PRESIDENT'S STATE VISIT
TO MEXICO

I call on you, Quetzalcoatl, Plumed Serpent,
uncoil like a stench of rotted fish and leather
from the dump heap of ancient tombs and altars,
uncoil like a vapor from a crack in the stoneworks,
from old prophecies and illuminated codices
and show this emperor the bird of smoke

                        twisting from his mirror;
trouble his naps between ghost-written speeches with dreams
of the bat which swoops down, blotting out the sun;
on goodwill tours, let him see nothing but that castrated youth
the priests have been feeding delicacies to
in perfumed chambers of the palace,
who breaks his flute in two and tears his white mantle
as he climbs the fifty odd lava steps to lie down

                        on the flat altar stone.
Let him move unguarded and pilotless out of his stateroom—
    out where only hands, delicate as a woman's, hold back
    the wall of flames moving up the woods;
let terrible lightning out of season and arrowhead clouds
    throw him face down in a field full of insects;
let him hear the barge of his stripped bones creak in the fallows;
let him wear a skin of green flies;
let fear fill up the empty space that was his guts
    and let his mind see the moment of its extinction—
    tyrannosaur, turtle, armor-plated Man;
let him shrink to an ant's antennae trembling
                in the lightest breeze rolling over a grassblade;

let the armies he has sent out swarm back to him;
let them crowd him out of his body, his house, his pockets;
let him stretch out under a glittering quilt of stars;
let there be rumors of his feet appearing in Asia,
     flying fish of his eyes
      leaping from the belly of the Atlantic.
For I have seen a vision: a lone car driving
     on a superhighway arched over dark space,
      heading straight into the eye of a squatting fly.

WORDS OVERHEARD IN AN
APPLE ORCHARD

Where are they, those ruddy pickers,
singing loudly to the mountains,
whose fingers move roughly
among the leaves, choosing us like heirs?

My skin is daily stretching
to the shape of a heart peaked with juices.
(Already the moon is a barrel of white cider.)
After two days, three at the most,
I'm sure to be caught here
with the look of a man surprised
to see his name on a weathered tombstone.

BACON'S VAN GOGH

Hunched over, it is walking
or standing still in the dark field.
Not a man wild for sun,
with glazed, green oriental eyes,
or hair so red
it lights up a whole wall;
not Theo's child or Gauguin's poor joke,
but a stick of coal, crude and hard
from the mines of Borinage,
made conscious of its heat.
No lover could be more alive.

A peasant's straw hat, or an ochre half-moon
of wax where a head would be,
comes almost to nothing.
Strapped to its back, a canvas stretched
large as the night.
There are no stars in it, not a one.

THE FOUNDRY

Between two sounds we are camped again—
A golden wickerwork of bird-calls
Touches the light of your face,
                    the different lights,
While the dull, daylong pounding
From the blackened foundry
Beats the air with a gloved fist. . . .
The same air that dries your hair
To a fragrance of honeysuckle, pounded
By those with the hideous gash across the eyebrow,
Who stare out at us
From beneath their goggles,
Terrible as skin-divers.

Like sluggish amphibians
From some inner darkness landward to die,
They emerge, line up
At the squat glowing forge.
They stand there, at noon, shelled
Gods in a stupor, never to be
Closer to the sun than now.
Night in the shape of a hammer
Falls and flattens them into sheet-metal.
In the flash,
They sneak their dead out
In the back of pick-up trucks,
The motor running.
The motors running.

Against them I see
What grows here, flowers at eye-level,
Whatever you take in your hands
Becoming the flesh of children,
Pure sound of tiger-lilies pitched so high
You make a hollow of your face
To catch it.

And the ocean it happens near . . .
As though we are drawn to this sea
Not because it is a mirror,
But a step.

III My Tropics

MY TROPICS

The red school lets out its children
stampeding as from a rodeo gate, slapping their thighs.
Day turns inward, brain-gray, and rains on
the young teacher, my age or younger, who looks at the sky,
tucks a notebook I wish were my head
to her breast, and turns the corner.

See the amber autolights on the gasoline
run with paper cutouts holding hands against the windows,
run with my youth that was sinuous as a barberpole—
each stripe a candycane, a road
(never one color for long), each twist boring a hole
to the pure, Platonic, sexless stratosphere
when I walked home from school through back lots
and "Keep Off" gardens, past the barbershop
alive with lime-plumed parakeets tweeting in cages,
hot towels so sweet with the odor of Barbasol, I'd stop
before the door and breathe deep till my scalp prickled.

Inside, overgrown jungle ferns spilled
from pots along the tile floor and darkwood shelves . . .
like the mud-choked Galapagos I wandered in,
but without those great hunched forms—part bird, part reptile,
their armor-plate and horns locked to the death—
that went crashing through the underbrush of my head.

The lofty chair, the riffling comb and scissors' cool glissade . . .
each stroke a bird-note to my ear!
Where are the plump fingers that smoothed the flush from my cheek
when rich curls rolled from my gown, thick and black;
when razorblade and sun shone as one,
my hothouse, my own, O my tropics!

FOR A GENTLEMAN WITH BLEACHED HAIR

You were the first gentleman I saw
in the cold. There would be more, later.
But your waste, threading drivel down your jaw,
comes home to me like pleurisy each winter.

Of all World War II's rationed, sick
years, I remember most the blizzard of '44;
you laid up, I swabbing you with Vicks,
then going back to my chemistry set. An in-law's
hand-me-down, an Arrow shirt, white on white,
swaddled your hair—frazzled
soul's one extravagance—
turned like mayonnaise left out too long,
botched like the smell and pallor of rotten eggs
from cheap miracle tints, your hair.

Alike even then, we both lived on
the landlady's Jewish dowry.
I was her son;
you (after you'd fathered me),
her segregated, spurned tenant.

One night, whimpering, cat-like, for a dish
of hot milk, you ran to the pantry. Cheeks flushed,
robe flailing about you like a tattered leash,
you bawled for attention, stamped and hammered and cursed
the lady of the house, and snatched your rent.
I'd never seen you so robust.

Later, told to go, you went.

Was that how you left London the day
Lloyd's nestegg cracked in the Depression—
to try again, to thaw and, at forty-one, to marry,
swear allegiance to a drafty room, a son,
and what life takes from those who cannot pay
for what they need? The poor get charity; you got none.
And that stack of health hints
clipped from the "News" each day, tied with shoe laces—
what good then, tucked like uncashed bonds in your drawer,
those free prescriptions for a bowel crisis!

As though my being born
was too much for the airless languor
you seemed to drift in like a diver's tank,
at forty-two, rather than risk any longer
coming up for air, you sank.

I left too, soon after.
Since then, I've learned to swim,
to hold my own a little better
than when mother dunked me in
a full tub, keeping my head under
to scare out my fear of water.
She made me learn how to clench and fight for breath,
but still, my breath.

Now, a later generation is priming
for its war to end all wars.
Late as usual yesterday, but not alone,
I went out where kids were snowballing
the fallen year, and bought a new lotion
to nurse back your lustrous hair.

HITCH-HIKER

Each man to his forced march; this is mine.
In the end everything runs out, runs
under the wheels—a bandage unwinding
on the centerline. Sometimes when my ribs clang
like a metal signpost at the edge of town,
and so much of the dark I cannot shut out
crawls with me into my sleeping bag,
I try to think where the owl goes.
For years now, my life has taken
no sharp turns, no climb, no detour,
but moves in neutral
down this smooth tar lane, one way.

The towns en route, the festooned, blazing towns,
are they dreams in my sleep, vanished
on waking? Even so, watching that white line
grow thin and luminous at night,
I feel the moon's hub unhinge from center
and roll berserk.

ARMOR

Helmet, that fit the peculiarities of my face
tight as a kid glove, these last years
have handled you so much, the imprint of my features
is worn down to a wax bullet.

Mouthpiece, visor, caparison that let me ride
through the dark towns of my ignorance
without seeing a thing,
you are no more a shield to me now
than my skin.

I'll miss you,
but missing is not quite the same as wanting.
If I'm to measure my estate before night falls,
I must give you up—if not heroically
like a lover then, slowly, one link at a time.

My heel gleams with a spur of light,
and the question I never asked occurs to me:
what freedoms must I have dragged behind
on a long leash, like a dog kept for amusement
who all along has been trotting beside me, speechless,
trying to tell me something?

WALKING ACROSS BROOKLYN BRIDGE

A black cat arching its back over the river
was how it looked that time, that first
time years ago, sailing out
from under. Behind me, hazy
as litter, freshly flushed, a string
of furnished rooms yawed
toward the Heights, the house
I couldn't love and gave up trying;
the cemetery next door, like a rough diamond
crystallizing, stone by crowning stone,
to a cutting-edge perfection,
where I used to walk, listening
for my own kind in the odd hours;
see my shadow, thin,
and bloated with moonlight, still too thin,
slipping through the bars, in and out,
stitching me in place.

Leaving was all I knew then. . . .

A stowaway sneaking brief, shallow breaths
under pitchblack tarpaulin,
his eye, a fingernail
picking at a patch of pale blue sky
big as a postage stamp,
trying to think what his rights were,
getting nowhere. . . .

Today, March twenty-first,
ten years, not too late, but later,
I walk across with the girl
you'd spoken against, who is my wife,
taking it all in:
light, through the Narrows' neck, unbottling,
erasing the shadow that circles me;
this bridge, sung to once
as a sort of lover or god.
And though I do not claim as much,
I can feel us breathing
great, reviving drafts of North Atlantic air,
the steel-ribbed diaphragm
humming like a harp.

Below us, taking their slow, sweet time,
three tugs drag in a tramper;
demurring, blistered down to waterline,
giving a toot for Liberty,
it keeps on coming in.
I would have you know,
in spite of our words, our silences,
and though I do not understand or love it,
I accept my life.

FOR KATHLEEN,
GONE ON A BRIEF JOURNEY

This, our first night apart,
the rain that falls
always without warning
on the seven deaf bridges of Paris
tossing beggars along like handbills
tonight spatters my shadow
with blue grease
till it runs, hatless, into the gutter.

All I can think of is
your comfort
my unkind words
your quick eyes
taking in a strange landscape,
how in two days
they'll flash evergreen
as you tell me what you saw:

loose among the dark pines of Alsace,
a golden bird—its long wings
beating for joy—
no man had seen or believed in
for a thousand years.

WALKING ON A CLEAR DAY

Spooned no drop of light
from last night's moon-ladle,
Oh city of sudden darkness
how you surprise me this morning!
The sunshine loving First Avenue
is hard to believe!
45° above, a wind pinching my toes,
God knows I'm the last
to compare you to Paris, bowl-blue,
when my sun-chair was a tulip's blossom.

The city is a cold river.
The city is a cold river flowing with fish.
The city is a cold river flowing with fish and scales
gleaming. I am a fish gleaming
scales from my pen, my silver ring, my belt-buckle;
from the bright brass key to my door;
from the clip of a large envelope in the mailbox containing a small
check;
from the aluminum trash basket that can't close its mouth on the
corner;
from the cracks in my old shoes wincing for a shine
to restore their original blackness;
from her northern hair, just washed, red as a tropical sunrise;
from the window-stripping of the Savings Bank
that guards not a nickel of mine;
from the rusted drinking fountain in the park;
from the park gate;
from the glinting whiskers of a bum peddling a tie at the entrance;

from the buttons of a brown suede coat launched
                              by a pretty girl down Eighth Street;
from a bubble of light shielding no one,
                              joyriding the top of a cab;
from the four Con Edison smokestacks of which only two are
                              smoking;
from my knuckles brushing her cheek just now;
from her cheek;
from the length of peeling bark on a maple tree;
from its dry leaves skittering
                              like the hooves of a splendid animal
                              moving westward to be born;
from an airliner's sparkling wing pinned to a laundry line;
from headlines tearing up in front of me and becoming birds;
from God's Adam's apple—the sun!
       I don't need to lift my head to hear what it's saying. . . .
Here, at eye-level, I kiss the warm throat this clear November day,
       bright scale, blue fish flowing in the cold river.

I HAD COME TO HOPE FOR SOMETHING

like the fawn-colored flanks
of that young mountain goat
                              leaping

over gray boulders—
pink hind legs scampering
downslope for cover
under the eyes of its mother,
the bus scattering the road,
butterflies, bugs, spattering the windows . . .

A quick glance of something wild—
    lord puma's sun pelt
        below rock-ledge

                              darting
    among cactus and shale flakes—
beauty not waiting for recognition . . .

And down further, the valley, red blooms
    and yellow braided jacaranda leaves
        yanked back, when I looked,
            into the muddy arroyo—

                              that too,

I had wanted to bring back
something of all that loveliness
                              glimpsed
        a moment, then gone—
to make something wild of our own—

58

something, whose father is fish
                whose mother is water,
after three months shaping
    in a darkness out of hand,
        is taken back,
                        wildly, like driftwood
        in the sea
        in the sea

LEAVING THE HOSPITAL

Like a fish to polluted water,
I cross the overpass and vault
a low iron fence eaten by river-rot.
I'm alone
as I'm ever likely to be in this city,
in the empty loading yard
of an abandoned sanitation plant.
Each peeled piling's shifty eye
is a gull watching me.
They strut there, above the current,
and take turns wheeling,
diving into the brownish flow
pumped out in wretched spasms
by two sewage pipes below.
I lean over the edge,
looking for a trace
of my unborn.
Turds skate out,
spinning like ice-skaters
at Rockefeller Center.
A tugboat's wake
breaks in huge, harmless V's along the barrier.

Under the plant-shed,
tonned totemic
steel mashers, grinders, ovens
gape vacantly as idiot prison guards
left without orders
from their warden

as to what to do
with the rows of new aluminum
wire-mesh trash baskets
lined up like empty cell-blocks.
Depression dulls
the scarred steel casing's
dented bald skulls.
Their fire has been dead for years,
but not their appetite.
Behind a concrete partition, a cop
catnaps like a baby, blue,
in the front seat of a patrol car,
a silver badge for a face.

Listen! The shriek of gull-gangs!
The unborn! The unburnable!
Against the swift surgical beaks
that dive and devour, devour and thrive—
cry, what cry?
Oh, say, like a boy, favorite among the elders,
who, with a silver pointer,
wove the strands of his voice
like David, into a slingshot
and hurled it
at the night sky's forehead. . . .
Mother, remember
how the rabbis, seated around the Talmud,
took another pinch of snuff and said
God Himself,
            for a moment,
turned from the stained-glass window—
            His shattered glass eye—

gleaming in slivers
on the dark streets of Warsaw,
turned even His ear
from the din in the dark streets of Warsaw
to hear my chant,
                    so sweet, so separate,
those years when prayer was fuel
for the pyres of Jews
unlucky enough not to be select,
Sephardic—like us—
those smelly Yiddish fish-peddlers
we'd thump our chests for at the altar,
but not invite to our table.

Now, not all the refined sugar
drifting in from the Domino factory
on the Long Island shore
can sweeten the least grief
for my likeness floating out of reach.
Oh, God of Abraham,
have you gone blind again, turning
against your own, your chosen . . . me!

A dot,
a tiny black dot, one
among millions in a news photo,
dilates, a pupil in the dark . . .
blackness multiplied by twos,
magnified to extinction!

I'm here. I'm still here.

Against this first unfinished death
of my body's light,
against the roadsign I turn to on the highway
that says DIE—
I have only the memory of a boy
in love with his voice
winding up God's ear-horn of birds.
The gulls have heard worse before, much worse;
have grown deaf from it,
and continue diving.

IN NO TIME

And if the full weight is not to be reasoned with,
nor lugged back up five flights
    and dumped in my father's lap,
under this leaky roof,
under trees fattening to a horizon of coal,
under a sky thin as a pregnancy,
under the scissor-lock buildings have me in,
    where I look up between their shiny legs,
under signs of a madness I have worked for,
under a churning that is not skin-deep,
    the dolphin in my belly wants to surface
    and sit up for the sun.
My sperm, like the sea, will touch all coastlines,
my throat vomit that cornered rodent,
who will pick himself up from the sand
and in no time execute a tapestry of footwork,
the envy of angels.

IV   Setting Out

SETTING OUT

I give my hand back to its place
    in the country of hands
I give my legs back to the road
My flowing sex I give to the Mother of Water
My hair to the mountain peak
I give my eye back to the head of the chestnut pony
The low spark at the tip of my spine
    I give to the backbone of stars
My sweat I give to the cloud
    moving toward the warm gulfstream
The letters of my name back to the Father of Alphabets
The dark cave under the outcrop of my forehead
    is making way for the prowlers of the sea
My lungs and ears and ambergris I give back to the wind
My sputtering desire to the more steadily burning sun
Not because it is all over
But that it might begin

BEARINGS

Skin transparent as water
a skylight for eyes
stars I see shining
on ripples of my belly
mountain stream fish swim in

Countries I enter enter me
my pores are nostrils
taking in scent of leaves and loam
of all I will soon be
Everglade swamp   pines of Reykjavik

That map
I crayoned over and over as a boy
trying to get it right   the greens and blues
then having to slog through on foot
was my body

Where I drew a river
deserts sometimes blow
and no bright bird will come to rest
I end somewhere beyond
those lights shifting red and blue

More transient of the two
I make my light
take in   disappear into
giving back world for world

THE ANGEL

If you don't hear from me again
pour sand in your clocks
and come close
to the bell of the color red

If you don't hear from me again
put your ear between the body
of the dog run down on the highway
and its mate, tongue out, panting over it

If you don't hear from me again
say love grew sick of waiting around
and kicked in the boarded-up windows
you stepped away from

If you don't hear from me again
go out on the road
that leads to the dangerous seasons . . .
the first sunbeam that touches you
that's it, that's all of love
lie down with it forever

If you don't hear from me again
close your books your passports
and look me up
in the red-hot dictionary of the sun

If you don't hear from me again
look out for that other who never blinks
who sees through you through everything

If you don't hear from me again
you are not listening

FOR A NEW HOUSE

Stirring in a place
I let others build for me,
I blink, get down from my shelf—
Throne or toilet, I never asked—
And where one word is as good as another,
In the dark,
Having no torch or lightning rod, I lift a finger,
And absence, like a pierced egg
Runs through the floorboards.
This bare, dank, starless body of a void opens house
To the infinite possibilities of love.

CHANGES

1.

Red circle
on blue square
To these particulars
the mind is
always
the late arrival

2.

Before sight
of anything—
death's flashcard

3.

You have swallowed
a bowl of vibrations
May you establish
in yourself
the highest wave
for praise

4.

Within me—
the serpent
without thickness

5.

Tributaries—
what I meant to say
coming together

6.

Nights rid of darkness
unusable witness
Only the word remains—
darkness

7.

Avocado, you are a sun
Tongue, you the earth
it rises over
and shines

8.

Dawn
emerging
like the unplugging
of an ear

9.

After a bath,
my slender foot
on the marble—
Egypt

10.

Bartok:
you are the sky
over jugglers, maypoles,
Chinese puppets, elephants,
Baltics, impenitent
Bluebeard

11.

My pubic hair—
ringlets on bath tiles,
ancient signature

12.

The humming of the yellow
and the humming of the black
meet
in the heart of the lily

13.

Shaggy mammoths
shake off their long sleep
in my throat,
tusks glistening,
trumpet
their sexual heat

14.

Your body is a field of snow
My fingers
make the first tracks

POEM

The sky is hung with shrouds
of Piranesi's dungeons,
and though I point to the spiral
birds uncorking the fog
that blocks a view of the harbor
on whose gleaming white shoulders
I have seen the vision steadily mount,
still she will not breathe me in.
The more I urge, the more she holds fast
to her ports of call, her limbs.
She wants a sign—thunder
in the middle of January; a mountain
turned into a golden bugle.
Just when everything is about time, she is afraid;
she wants to drag the planet along
like a rag doll.
            I want to say, "But it's you
who has pried loose
the NO at the base of my spine;
the wrongs done to me, and by me,
set in a row of discs running up my back."
Memory, gravity, are easing now,
and I can feel a song in me
blowing together like a flock of birds
against the sky, a sheet of music,
and my spirit rounding, swelling
to fit one of the clusters flying by.

I am going out
as far as the sound of galactic sifting
to bring back legends
I have made up
against the gods of darkness.
Then will you breathe me in?

THE VISIT

How to deal with it, shuddering house
    siding with downfall,
myself, the wall I am
    flattened against;
balls and bowels
    wrung like a neck;
what do or make of you,
    guest, Elijah, death,
sucking me dry
    through the straw
of my body; yes,
I had prepared a place,
    that place was me;
but near all eaten now,
    face to face,
you are not so strange,
    what fear made . . .
you *are* my fear, other
    side of my face
I didn't look at; fear
    that increased
as my power to feel
    you increased . . .
I cast you out!

What's left
is my power
    that made you, death,
with my face coming
    and going, like water,
where I begin,
    What's left
will come out of this
    no house, no
ear to the ground, but
    slung low and swaying,
roofless
    as a bridge.

LIGHT POEM

The light without a body
without skin   without bones or veins
without feet   without hands
is strong, but lightly
the light has no wants
still the field flowers
when he comes out of nowhere
light is in the wood   in the water
without youth   without age   without old age
though he is seen
he was not born   he does not die
he is early   he is late
he will not come when we wish him
he walks on the hillside in summer
he walks on the snow
he is naked   he wears the seasons for clothes
he is there with our enemies
here with our friends
he is silent   he sings
he comes from the heat of the sun
the coolness of the moon

GOING OUT TO MEET THE SUN IN A TIME OF DARKNESS

Lost in a darkness too much like his father's,
my father lives under the wheels
of a gypsy caravan pitched by the river.
I have gone off with their daughter,
leaving behind a pile of the ancestral letter M
in neat, even mountain ranges.

Laid out flat, the roads and woods
are stacks of sweetness I walk
on the two breezes of my legs.
Her lightness is teaching me to become an odor.

What's left of the sea is
a blue stain at the roof of my mouth;
and death is a drop of water
drying on the tongue.
No deck I have imagined is bigger than my eye
rolling to bring her into focus.

And each night, when the sun falls into the river
and changes into the bloated carcass of a horse
gangs of boys run out to stone,
on all fours we steal out
to the high marsh grass and look
for the white horse
that will be the rising sun,
and becoming one of its rays, silently
worship him.

YOU ARE WATER

Now all in the curled flower you held to like breath,
bidden, rises as pollen.
Petals, fragile empires, and calyx gone up in summer's blue smoke.
Where it goes to is not yours yet.
What remains is no one's.

Fermenting in the purple sex of the grape,
the dream of hardest crystal.
It feeds on pain, the only fire that still nourishes.
Why should you have believed otherwise?
On what star's face did you read it?

Once the children of heroes combed women out of foam and sunlight.

For their enemies they hewed
an alphabet of spears.
Now they cannot tell the difference between beauty and fear.
While they sleep, the earth kneels
offering the wound in its neck to a humorless moon
which washes down its dinner with the doused fire of the sea.
A calm, insatiate hunger, the equal of time's,
feeds on the whites of your eyes.

Prowler, whatever roots you feared you would shrivel without—
Look!—they shrivel without you.
Let them.
You are water.

REMAINS

1.

Prematurely, practically in mid-ocean,
The Pacific's grueling waves
Begin breaking more than a hundred yards out.
Perhaps this is a more accurate graph
Of the soundwaves, barely audible,
Faltering like a stutterer's next syllable
From the opposite shore. . . .
As if wrangling centuries
Falling all over their watery outlines
Cannot wait to be the first to my rescue!

2.

The sea's blank face
Is a clock.
Its hands are so polished
With the sheen of the present
They are nowhere visible in the steady throbbing.
Vast, unlinear,
Porous as a web,
The sea must remember everything.
Now I know
That what I have been dreading most
Is not death, but forgetfulness.

3.

From flashing windows,
Concrete blockhouses above the dunes seem to be
The white nests
Of huge bronze birds
Carved from polar light.
But when they come down,
The birds are so comically small and fragile,
Cartoons of fury
With black circles under the eyes,
And thin Proustian bills
They will dip gingerly as straws
Through patches of mudflats,
A silvery
Broken jigsaw of remembrances in the distance—
Like the pages
Of a book no earthly glue can hold together.
How I envy the sun
Continually burning its books!

4.

Walking,
I come upon something
The ocean has put off taking back to itself,
Like the cruel, prolonged subtleties
Of a practical joke.
From the limp flipper
Tucked coyly as a faggot's wrist at the waist,
It must be the remains of a sea-lion.

How minutely
Guts and muscles shred and topple
Like a sodden ball of India hemp.
Each soft nibble of the tide
Savors, cuts closer to the bone
That gave this wreckage a backbone against time.
The curved ribs are visible, bare.
No longer are they trying to snag
A keepsake from the air, the live
Chaotic
Open heart of space.

5.

For an instant, a blob of foam
Scurries up the shortening ladder of the spinal column,
Teeters there,
Iridescent bubble
Within whose dizzying round wall
The suspended breath of the day revolves.
Like antlers, the upswept ribcage shines in the cold froth.
Wherever I look,
Light deepens, digs in
Between onrushing waves.

ABOUT THE AUTHOR

Jack Marshall was born and brought up in Brooklyn and has traveled, lived and worked in several parts of the world: as a deckhand on a ship to Africa; in Europe, in a vineyard outside Barcelona; in Mexico; and on the Lower East Side in New York. Most recently he has lived in San Francisco with his wife and young son. This year he is teaching at the University of Iowa Poetry Workshop.

Format by Katharine Sitterly
Set in Intertype Weiss
Composed and printed by York Composition Co., Inc.
Bound by The Haddon Craftsmen, Inc.
HARPER & ROW, PUBLISHERS, INCORPORATED

69 70 71 72 73 10 9 8 7 6 5 4 3 2 1